WHAT WAS IT LIKE?

when your grandparents were your age

by

Ann Cook, Marilyn Gittell & Herb Mack

PANTHEON BOOKS

Our thanks to:

Jackie Ancess, Frankie
and Bob Borzello, Elinor Bowles, Lenore Coral,
Laurie Indenbaum, Charlotte LaRue, Harriet Parker, Mary Frances Rhymer,
Christine Schelshore, Natalie Seweryn,
Leslie Stein, and George Talbot.

Front cover photograph,
courtesy of the Weinberger family.
Title page photograph,
State Historical Society of Wisconsin.

Library of Congress Cataloging in Publication Data
Cook, Ann, 1940-
What was it like? when your grandparents were your age
SUMMARY: Text and more than one hundred photographs
describe life in the United States during the 1920's and 30's.
1. United States—Social life and customs—1918-1945—Juvenile
literature. [1. United States—Social life and customs—1918-1945]
I. Gittell, Marilyn, joint author. II. Mack, Herb, 1937-
joint author. III. Title.
E169.C747   973.91   75-35893
ISBN 0-394-82993-X
ISBN 0-394-92993-4 lib. bdg.

DESIGNED BY SALLIE BALDWIN/SPENCER DRATE
Manufactured in the United States of America
First Edition

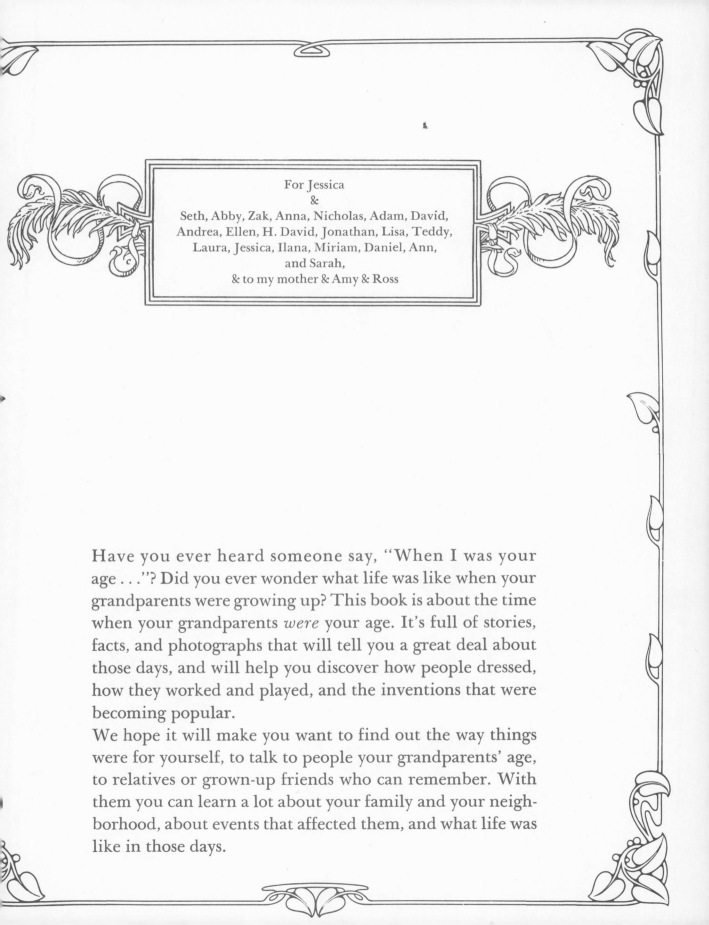

For Jessica
&
Seth, Abby, Zak, Anna, Nicholas, Adam, David,
Andrea, Ellen, H. David, Jonathan, Lisa, Teddy,
Laura, Jessica, Ilana, Miriam, Daniel, Ann,
and Sarah,
& to my mother & Amy & Ross

Have you ever heard someone say, "When I was your age . . ."? Did you ever wonder what life was like when your grandparents were growing up? This book is about the time when your grandparents *were* your age. It's full of stories, facts, and photographs that will tell you a great deal about those days, and will help you discover how people dressed, how they worked and played, and the inventions that were becoming popular.

We hope it will make you want to find out the way things were for yourself, to talk to people your grandparents' age, to relatives or grown-up friends who can remember. With them you can learn a lot about your family and your neighborhood, about events that affected them, and what life was like in those days.

COLLECTION OF CORAL FAMILY

COLLECTION OF MASON FAMILY

NEW YORK PUBLIC LIBRARY, SCHOMBURG COLLECTION

You may find it hard to imagine that the children you see here are now your grandparents' age. They have gone to school, worked, married, and raised families—perhaps they are now retired.

As you look closely at these pictures, you'll find clues that tell you they were taken many years ago—details like the clothes people are wearing, the hair styles, or the kinds of toys the children are playing with.

You may be able to tell that the pictures were taken long ago by the way people are posed or by the objects in the background.

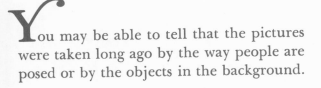

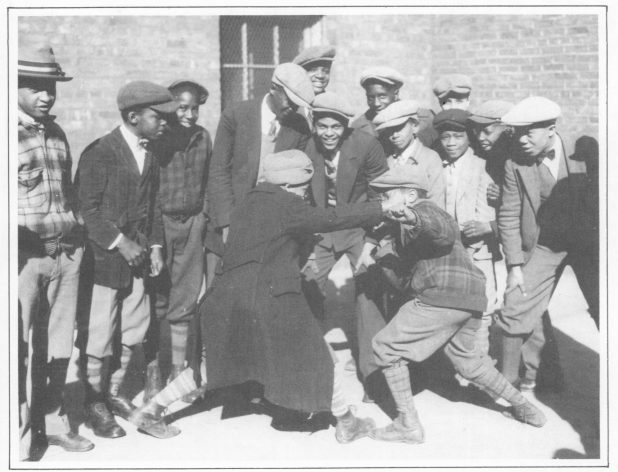

You'll have to look at many different photos to get a good idea of what life was like when your grandparents were your age. Some of the pictures in this book might make you think that children in those days always stood around in their best clothes with their hair neatly combed, but as you look at many pictures you'll quickly see this isn't true.

You may enjoy asking yourself questions about the photos. Some questions, like "why is that water fountain shaped so strangely?" may have simple answers. Others you'll just have to guess at, like "how thick would the trunk of that skinny tree be today if it were still alive?"

Perhaps you'll be curious about who took a particular photograph and whether or not the people shown realized it was being taken.

COLLECTION OF GEISMAN FAMILY

Old school photographs are a good place to search for clues to the past. If you have a recent class photograph of your own, see if it looks like the ones you see here.

In your grandmother's time some children went to a one-room schoolhouse where children of all ages and grades were taught by the same teacher. Schools were also places where children did sewing, played field hockey, and had fingernail inspections and milk breaks.

MUSEUM OF THE CITY OF NEW YORK, JACOB RIIS COLLEC

NEW YORK PUBLIC LIBRARY, SCHOMBURG COLLECTION

When your grandmother was young, only four out of ten children her age went to high school. And only about one of those four actually graduated. Most children were working full-time by the time they were fifteen. Today, more than nine out of every ten children go to high school, and most graduate. Usually people today don't begin to work in full-time jobs until they are nineteen or older.

Your own grandparents might have worked before or after school, and couldn't join their friends in games until their jobs or chores were finished. Many worked to help their parents pay for food or housing.

Boys worked as assistants to people like the iceman, the junkman, the milkman, or the ice-cream man. They earned anywhere from twenty-five to forty cents for a full day's work—which often meant starting at seven in the morning and finishing up at five or six in the evening. Boys who worked as Western Union messengers were some-times teased by their friends, who called the boys' uniforms "women's underwear."

Because there were no home deliveries, newsboys—some of them only eight years old—were a common sight on city street corners. For selling two-cent newspapers every afternoon from three-thirty to seven, they could earn twenty-five cents.

Children who didn't have to work after school could play with friends. Vacant lots, backyards, a special fishing pond or swimming hole—these were popular places to meet. After a heavy rainstorm, some lots became wonderful wading ponds. In those days it was easy to find vacant lots on which to play. They were usually pieces of unused land that had never had any buildings on them. Many areas near cities were still farms or ranches where your grandparents may have played when they were children. Now most of these farms and ranches have become parts of the city. The land your own house is built on might have been a vacant lot or even a farm when your grandmother

was your age. With some good detective work, you might be able to find out the history of your own neighborhood—how many buildings have been built on a particular piece of land and what those buildings were like.

The goat might make you wonder what pets children had, or whether all the animals around the house were really pets. Laws may have been different then regarding what animals could be kept in a city.

Many of the games children played were the same as those played today—games like kick the can, marbles, baseball, football, hop scotch, jackstones (jacks), johnny on the pony, hide and seek, jumprope, follow the leader. These games often began as soon as school was out and lasted until it grew dark or dinner was ready.

Chants of *Ole Ole Ocean Free* and *Finders Keepers, Losers Weepers* could be heard wherever children played in the streets. Some kids made a game of skipping along the sidewalk, saying,

> *Step on a crack*
> *You'll break your mother's back.*

They sang other skipping or ball-bouncing rhymes too, such as,

> *One, two, three, four*
> *Charlie Chaplin went to war,*
> *He taught the ladies how to dance*
> *and this is what he taught them*
> *Heel, toe, over you go,*
> *Heel, toe, over you go;*
> *Salute to the king*
> *And bow to the queen,*
> *And turn your back*
> *On the submarine.*

And when it rained, children sang,

> *It's raining, it's pouring*
> *The old man is snoring*
> *He got into bed*
> *And bumped his head*
> *And couldn't get up in the morning.*

Try making a collection of the word games you have heard and see whether these games differ from the ones that were popular when your grandparents were growing up.

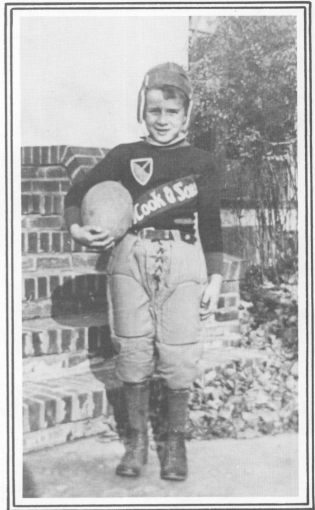

COLLECTION OF ZABAN FAMILY

On a rainy day, or during a long Sunday afternoon, children often played indoors with friends or relatives who came to visit. Some indoor games that were popular in those days were Parcheesi, dominoes, lotto, checkers, tic-tac-toe, and dots.

MUSICAL ROCK-A-BYE CRADLE

TRIMMED CARRIAGE

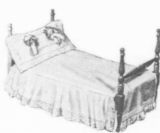

DOLL'S BED

MUSICAL ROCK-A-BYE CRADLE

No. G-8917—Rock-a-bye baby on a tree-top"—it sweetly plays lulling Dolly to slumber—and what dolly could resist with such inducement. A darling cradle and it's tall 13½" long inside—perfect for our Patsy Babykin. Strongly made in natural finish maple with rockers and all and completely fitted with a comfy mattress, a pillow and a pretty ruffly cover all of gay-flowered cretonne. Music box winds underneath............... $7.50

TRIMMED CARRIAGE FOR PATSY BABYKIN

No. AA-8911/1—Dolly will look just too sweet peering out from under the "beribboned" hood of this dainty carriage. See the pretty robe that comes with it, made of silk moire with a big satin bow, there's a matching pillow all nice and fluffy and a soft mattress too so Dolly will be comfy. Carriage is entirely constructed of wood brightly enameled and the hood is convertible. Measures 20" to handle; 15" x 8½" inside, just fits Patsy Babykin. Pink or Blue............... $6.00

No. A-563—Our own Patsy Babykin in long pink or blue trimmed dress, cap and booties. 10" high.............. $3.25

DOLLS' BEDS

No. B-8/100—(illustrated) Dolly's "four poster" of solid wood nicely enameled. Of course you can't see the nice mattress or the long fluffy pillow but it is there, and two crispy white sheets and case and a soft blanket too. The spread is made over a pink or blue foundation and lace-trimmed, the matching bolster cover has satin bows. Trimming in Pink or Blue; 18" bed in maple or green. State colors............... $4.25

No. B-8/200—Same but 23½" long in Pink or Blue trimming, bed in maple or green. State colors............. $6.50

No. C-8/100—18" bed only, maple or green............ $1.75

No. C-8/200—23½" bed only, maple or green............ $3.00

SO DOLLY CAN SLEEP OR TAKE THE AIR IN STYLE

NEW IDEAS IN TRAFFIC TOYS

MOST OF THEM EXCLUSIVELY MADE FOR F. A. O. SCHWARZ

DOUBLE DECKER

"DOUBLE DECKER"

No. K-718—This mechanical "double decker" has plenty of room inside with long side seats on both decks and stairs to reach the top. It operates by a strong, clock winding motor and carries a standard batttery for its electric headlights. Large double rear wheels keep the bus steady. Smartly painted in red and yellow with black lines. Driver at wheel. Measures 14" long and 7" high. $2.50

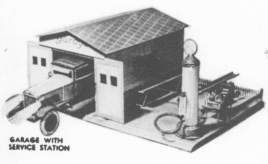

GARAGE WITH SERVICE STATION

FIRE CHIEF AUTO

TRAFFIC LIGHT

GARAGE WITH SERVICE STATION

No. L-564/46—Just run the 13" red and tan mechanical car with 2 electric headlights and gas tank which can be filled up to the gas station for service or park it in the garage. Car has clock winding motor. The garage itself, 9" high, is painted cream with green trim and red roof. Wide sliding door. The car lifter in the sand-colored yard is elevated by means of a handle. The red and white gas pump has valve at back and the gas first rises in the glass before it flows out of the hose. Table with red oil can and four bottles. All metal, 14" x 19" overall. Our own design $10.00

FIRE CHIEF AUTO WITH SIREN

No. K-266—Gangway—the siren screams realistically— here comes the Fire Chief! A perfect miniature of a completely equipped fire car—brilliantly enameled in flashy red and black with shiny nickel finish head and tail lights that flare out either bright or dim in the dark— solid rubber tires that grip the road for safe speeding— and an automatic siren that screeches its warning while the car is in action. Strong clock motor adjusted by brake. All batteries included. Length 14". Special low Christmas price $1.50

ELECTRIC TRAFFIC LIGHT

No. J-1/186—The lights are always right when you have your own traffic tower. Made of metal, 8" high, with gray base and green column, red and green lights on all four sides just like a real street signal. Switch to automatically operate. Complete, with battery.............. $3.75

745 - FIFTH AVENUE at 58TH ST. N.Y.

Page 47

Then, as now, children could choose to do many things. Your grandparents may have taken part in religious activities, enjoyed the visits of the public library bookmobile, or gone to the regular scout meeting or an outing. Perhaps on special occasions they went to the zoo, took a pony ride, went

STATE HISTORICAL SOCIETY OF WISCONSIN

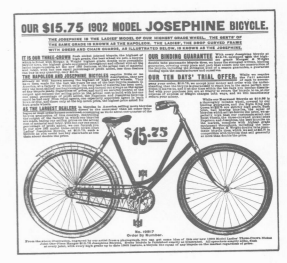

NEW YORK PUBLIC LIBRARY PICTURE COLLECTION

CHICAGO HISTORICAL SOCIETY

to the beach or for a day's drive in the family car.

Some of the things your grandparents did are no longer done today. Your grandmother might have danced around a maypole at a spring festival. This custom began long ago. Now the maypole has almost disappeared.

The girls dressed in costumes may look like they are trick-or-treating for Halloween. But when your grandparents were young, children dressed up on Thanksgiving. They went around asking for money, saying, "Anything for Thanksgiving?"

Of course, your grandparents did other things when they were your age. To find out what some of them were, you might start by guessing. Later, you may be surprised by what people tell you.

CHICAGO HISTORICAL SOCIETY

PARIS DESIGNERS ACCEPT BERTHAS AND RUFFLES

4856—A bertha
effect and the flari
add a demure qua
to this sleeveless
frock. Designed fo
12 to 38. Size 16 i
3¼ yards 39-inch
Width about 2⅝

One of the things people always remember best is their wedding. What stories can they tell you about it? How much do you think a bride's dress cost? Where do you think couples went on honeymoons?

You might be surprised to find out that many couples didn't have a honeymoon, or if they did, they stayed only one night in a local hotel. Most people did not have enough money to do much more. Those couples who did have a little money went to special spots, like Niagara Falls.

An entire wedding in the 1920s, including hiring of a hall and serving food, might

MATTHEW WITT, STATE HISTORICAL SOCIETY OF WISCONSIN

have cost about $25. Guests enjoyed sandwiches, peanuts, soft drinks, and cake. Sometimes money was given as a wedding present. A gift of $5 was considered generous, though $2 was more usual.

"Courting" couples would often take a walk or go to a café to sit and talk over a cup of coffee and perhaps a piece of pie. Someone lucky enough to have a friend with a car could drive around town looking for others who were out "motoring."

Dating couples also went on picnics and spent evenings at home singing and playing the piano.

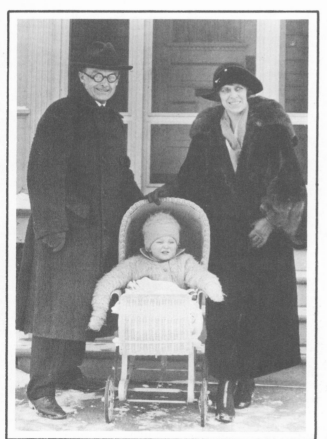

Families were often larger in those days. It wouldn't have been unusual for your grandfather or grandmother to have had six or seven brothers and sisters.

As you look at these children with their families, you can see some objects—the baby carriage, for example—that have changed a lot. Making up stories about the children you see in these photographs might interest you. What do you think they are doing now? What do you think their childhood was like?

When you look at the large farm family standing under the tree, try and guess how all the different people were related. Large families like this one provided the hands necessary to do all the work. Today, most of that work is done by machines.

In your grandparents' time, just as in our own, the amount of money a family

had made a difference in the way they lived.

Homes were usually heated by a wood-burning stove. But, for some people, wood was too expensive to burn only for heating. So the stove was also used to warm an iron, dry clothing, cook a meal, and heat the water for a bath.

What you already know can help you think about the pictures you see. Americans came to this country from many different lands. In one of the pictures you can see two flags in the background. From this you may be able to figure out where the family came from.

How much do you know about your own family? By looking at family photographs and talking with your relatives, you may discover some interesting facts.

If you ask good questions, the answers will probably be more rewarding. For example, instead of just finding out who married whom, you might ask how the couples met. Instead of finding out what people did, try to find out what they thought about their work.

When your grandparents were growing up, one special event was a family trip to the clothing store. New clothes were usually bought for special occasions, like weddings or holidays.

Some of the clothes that were the very latest style in those days might look a bit strange to you today. But other clothing might look familiar because over the years fashions go out of style and then become popular again.

Women's clothes, especially, have changed a lot.

The clothes people wore in those days may seem unsuitable to us today. How good a game of tennis could you play, or how fast a race could you run, dressed as people are here?

Your grandmother might have felt uncomfortable in these sport clothes, yet she wore them because she might have thought other things were more important than comfort. Or she may have considered them a big improvement from the past.

CHICAGO HISTORICAL SOCIETY

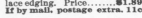

No. 38R714 A
beautiful Marguerite
combination chemise,
made of fine nain-
sook; trimmed around
neck with narrow lawn
ruffle which is edged
with fine torchon lace,
insertion of ribbon;
twenty rows of fine
torchon lace insertion
(ten rows on each side)
reaching from neck to
waist, and edging on
each side to match;
fine embroidery in-
sertion at waist with
ribbon insertion;
eight clusters of fine
tucks (three rows in a
cluster) in back from
neck to waist; has a
wide flounce at bottom,
three rows of tucks;
ruffle with torchon
lace edging. Price........$1.89
If by mail, postage extra, 11c

NEW YORK PUBLIC LIBRARY PICTURE COLLECTION

laces that were familiar to your grand-parents when they were growing up look very different today. Even some that may seem the same at first glance were really quite different. There were grocery stores, ice-cream parlors, hamburger joints, and automats. Notice any differences? Look at the furniture, the decorations, the lighting, and the way the napkins are stacked. All these details tell you something about how life has changed.

There wasn't any air conditioning in those days, as the ceiling fans in the automat should tell you. Many other modern conveniences weren't available then, either.

Some treats, like ice-cream sodas, were old traditions by the time your grand-parents were your age. People say that about a hundred years ago, a man was serving a popular drink made of sweet cream, syrup, and carbonated water. When he ran out of cream, he substituted vanilla ice cream. The new drink became so popular it spread across the country.

Dancing every evening 6:30 P. M. to 1:00 A. M.
in the Blue Fountain Room
"HUSK" O'Hare and His Band

Cover Charge 50c Per Person
Saturdays $1.00 Per Person
After 9:00 P. M.

Hotel La Salle
85c Luncheon
FROM 11:30 A. M. TO 2:30 P. M

CHOICE OF
Supreme of fresh fruit, Favorite

Fresh shrimp cocktail   Tunafish canape
Consomme Julienne peluche

Old-fashioned potato soup with leeks

CHOICE OF
Fried silver smelts, sauce tartare, au gratin potatoes

Black sea bass saute Meuniere, Monaco, pommes Gaufrette

Scrambled eggs with goose liver and mushrooms saute au Madere

Braised short ribs of beef with fresh vegetables Bourgeoise
pommes rissole

Minced chicken and Virginia ham with mushrooms
green peppers, poached egg au gratin

Broiled end of beef tenderloin steak, coquelicot, pommes noisette

La Salle special vegetarian luncheon with poached egg

Roast fricandeau of veal, macaroni au gratin, pommes persilie

BLUE-PLATE SPECIAL
Smoked frankfurter sausage with sauerkraut, pommes nouvelle

Cold: Pickled lamb tongue with string bean salad

CHOICE OF
Apple or grape-nut custard pie   Farina pudding, fruit sauce
Biscuit Frascatti   Special macaroon cake   Raspberry water ice
Sliced bananas with cream   Home-style peaches with cake
Strawberry, chocolate or coffee ice cream
Cottage cheese with raspberry preserves

Gluten bread   Single portion of bread and butter included
CHOICE OF
Tea, coffee, chocolate, milk or buttermilk

Heart of romaine and beet salad (15c) extra
French or Thousand Island dressing

February 28, 1931

In those days there were no supermarkets. Instead, there were butcher shops, vegetable stands, fish stores, and groceries. At the grocery a clerk took the order and got the items down from the shelf. There were no self-service carts and goods were stacked behind the counters. What difference do you think this would make in the way people shopped? Find out what someone who lived then thinks about today's supermarkets.

Prices are one change you're sure to keep noticing. The dresses, chairs, drugstore items, cars, soft drinks, even the rifles and banjoes you see in these pictures, would be very inexpensive if we could buy them now for the prices they were then.

After a long, dusty ride, there's nothing like a glass of

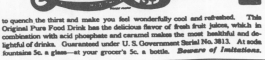

to quench the thirst and make you feel wonderfully cool and refreshed. This Original Pure Food Drink has the delicious flavor of fresh fruit juices, which in combination with acid phosphate and caramel makes the most healthful and delightful of drinks. Guaranteed under U. S. Government Serial No. 3813. At soda fountains 5c. a glass—at your grocer's 5c. a bottle. *Beware of Imitations.*

PEPSI COLA COMPANY

SEARS ROEBUCK AND COMPANY PICTURE COLLECTION

In 1922 toothpaste sold for thirty-one cents a tube, and a good shopper could find a summer dress for forty-eight cents! But when your grandparents were growing up, people complained about prices just as they do today. How come?

The answer begins with how much money people can earn in their work and how much they can afford to spend.

Take groceries, for example:

	1919	1975
Quart of milk	$ .15	$ .45
Dozen eggs	.68	.70
Bread	.10	.32
Pound of pork chops	.42	1.67
Pound of bacon	.55	1.57
Dozen oranges	.53	1.30
	$2.44	$6.01

From this list, it's easy to see that food cost a lot less in 1919 than it did in 1975.

But does that mean it was cheaper? In 1919 people earned an average of only 47 cents an hour, while in 1975 the average was $4.44 an hour. So in 1919 it would have taken your greatgrandfather about five hours of work to buy this list of groceries. In 1975, someone would have had to work less than an hour and a half to buy the same list.

With this in mind, you can see that things like toothpaste, dresses, fish, Kleenex, and cars weren't so cheap after all.

NASH

Leads the World in Motor Car Value

Special Six Coupé

A Superb New Nash Model

Admirably Designed for Business or Shopping

...osely created ...s of com-

...art ...y

nickeled radiator shell.

The interior is rendered attractive with Gray-Green Duotone genuine leather upholstery. And the fittings and appointments are of select calibre and completeness.

Particularly is the brisk and spirited character of its supremely smooth, quiet performance of notable interest.

And included *at no extra cost* among the car's outstanding mechanical features are four-wheel brakes, full balloon tires, five disc wheels, air cleaner, gas filter and an oil purifier.

...TORS COMPANY
...a, Wisconsin   (3165)

CHEVROLET

How to buy a Chevrolet *with* $5 down

You probably never have heard of some of the cars that were popular when your grandparents were your age, but one car you may know—a Model T Ford. It cost $775 in 1920. For only $25 more, people could buy an electric self-starter, so they didn't have to crank the engine by hand to start it.

FORD MOTOR COMPANY

COLLECTION OF THE LIBRARY OF

AUTHOR'S COLLECTION

Today we take for granted many inventions like the pop-up toaster and the shower. But these caused great excitement when your grandparents were growing up, and some, like the permanent hairwaving machine, were even modeled by celebrities like Miss America. The new inventions look strange to us now, even though their names are very familiar.

Top-Left Advertisement

Now Comes — Simplified
Electric Refrigeration

THE CREATION OF GENERAL ELECTRIC—
THE LEADING RESEARCH ORGANIZATION OF THE WORLD

THE GENERAL ELECTRIC ICING UNIT
is the revolutionary feature of new-day refrigeration.

Outstanding Advantages

Simplified—no pipes, no drains, no attachment. Portable—install anywhere. Just plug into nearest electric outlet and it starts.

Quiet—three feet away you can hardly hear it.

No Servicing—never needs oiling or attention. All moving parts are enclosed in an hermetically sealed housing.

Economical—uses very little current and maintains uniform temperature.

Clean—the circulation of air through the coils draws dust away from the top of the refrigeration.

Guaranteed by General Electric

THERE is now a new development in electric refrigeration for the home. An amazingly simplified icing unit by General Electric Company. A factor everyone, from now on, must take into account when considering an electric refrigerator. Electric refrigeration—above all things an *electrical* problem—has been solved *electrically* by the world's outstanding group of technical experts.

The General Electric icing unit is so supremely engineered and so precisely constructed that its operation is practically noiseless three feet from the refrigerator. It uses very little current and no special wiring is needed to hook it up—the regular house circuit is adequate.

The entire mechanism is housed in an hermetically sealed casing mounted on top of the cabinet. You *never* need oil it—*never* need touch it. It operates automatically, maintaining a *practically constant* temperature in the refrigerator.

Only an institution like General Electric Company—with its world-wide electrical resources—could have produced so outstanding an electrical achievement.

It marks 15 years of intensive research. Some 64 leading engineers cooperated in its development. Their goal was to produce the *simplest, most practical* electric refrigerator Electrical Science could achieve. Several thousand refrigerators—of 19 different designs—were built, field-tested and improved before production of the models now announced, was authorized. They embody the best thought of the leading electrical research organization of the world.

Now thousands who have deferred the purchase of electric refrigeration will want to see this new creation, will wish to find out what General Electric has done in the field. Buying any other way is a mistake.

The General Electric Refrigerator is obtainable in various sizes suitable for every home. Different models are now on display at lighting companies and dealers everywhere.

Write for Booklet No. 6-A. It tells all about this new-day refrigerator.

Electric Refrigeration Department
of General Electric Company
Hanna Building, Cleveland, Ohio

GE Refrigerator

GENERAL ELECTRIC

[1927]

AUTHOR'S COLLECTION

Top-Right Advertisement

"As Safe As Electric Light"   "A Child Can Operate Them"

Begin Your Collection of this beautiful
Thermo-Electric Ware with the

General (GE) Electric
Radiant Toaster

Make Crisp, Delicious, Golden-Brown Toast on the Breakfast Table

The four spiral coils of wonderful "Calorite" wire get red hot in a few seconds. With this *radiant* heat you can make a slice of toast a minute for 1-10 of a cent a slice.

This toaster lasts a lifetime. All toasters are thoroughly tested before shipment.

On a severe life test one G-E Toaster remained in perfect working order for 13,875 hours. This toaster—making 10 slices of toast for every breakfast—would have lasted one family over 225 years. It was a regular stock toaster.

Accept no substitute.

If you cannot get it from your lighting company, electrical supply dealer, or from the department and hardware stores selling similar household appliances, write us.

For $4.50 we will deliver prepaid through our nearest representative, one toaster complete with rack and attaching plug. With hand decorated base, shown above, $1.00 extra.

Be sure to state the voltage of your electric lighting circuit.

General Electric Company

Largest Electrical Manufacturer in the World

Dept. 39-H   Schenectady, N. Y.

2932

Our Money-Back Guarantee insures every advertisement

Bottom-Left Advertisement

Monarch
Electric Ranges

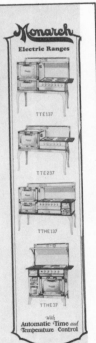

TTE137

TTE237

TTHE137

TTHE37

with
Automatic Time *and* Temperature Control

A Delicious Baked Ham With Cinnamon Apples

(Recipe furnished on request)

What an appetizing meal it suggests—think of what little it would take to complete the menu with this attractive service for the main course—and it does not require difficult or elaborate preparations, especially with a MONARCH oven equipped with Automatic Time and Temperature Controls—no oven watching is necessary, after the food is once placed in the oven you are relieved of all responsibility until the meal is to be served.

The wonderful convenience and efficiency of cooking electrically is being realized more every day and with the MONARCH's many fuel saving features it is economical too—call on your local MONARCH dealer or write us direct, we will be glad to furnish you further information regarding this modern kitchen equipment and its many advantages.

MONARCH ELECTRICS HAVE BEEN APPROVED BY

National Board of Fire Underwriters   Good Housekeeping Institute
Wisconsin Power and Light Company
and many other leading Utility Companies

Manufactured by

MALLEABLE IRON RANGE COMPANY
Beaver Dam, Wisconsin

Makers of the famous MONARCH Coal-Wood Range. Now manufacturing a complete line of cooking devices.

Monarch
Coal-Wood and Electric

Paramount
Gas and Combination Ranges

AUTHOR'S COLLECTION

Bottom-Right Advertisement

MARCHAND'S Golden Hair Wash will bring back the golden hue to naturally blonde hair that has become darkened. It will also transform black or brown hair to beautiful auburn or chestnut tints, and if lighter or golden shades are desired, applications are repeated until the result is achieved.

The method of producing these charming colorful tints requires no degree of skill. Results are secured quickly, easily and safely, and are not affected by washing or shampooing. Marchand's Golden Hair Wash has been a favorite with French hairdressers in New York for over thirty years.

MARCHAND'S
GOLDEN HAIR
WASH

The HOOVER

1908 - *Twenty Years of Progress* - 1928

THE HOOVER COMPANY

CHICAGO HISTORICAL SOCIETY

$6.65 Floor Polishing Outfit — $5.00

This outfit is just the thing for waxing the floors and linoleum in homes and small offices. It consists of:

1 Quart Johnson's Liquid Wax . $1.40
1 Johnson lamb's-wool Wax Mop   1.50
1 Johnson Weighted Floor
  Polishing Brush 3.50
1 Johnson Book on Home
  Beautifying 25
                              $6.65
A Saving of $1.65!

Some machines just didn't exist in those days. The dryer, for instance, has replaced the clothes line. Other changes might seem unimportant, but they made a big difference to some people. The bulky wheelchair in the photograph, which made it difficult to travel, has been replaced by a lightweight, collapsible one.

Many people have said that progress ended some good things, such as a visit from the iceman. He used to come regularly to put a large chunk of ice into an insulated wooden box. This "icebox" kept food cool in the days before the electric refrigerator. With the invention of this appliance, the iceman's job became unnecessary. The milkman, the diaper man, and the coal man are still around, but we see them less and less often. Do you think these changes have made life easier or more pleasant? It's a hard question, and people disagree about the answer.

STATE HISTORICAL SOCIETY OF WISCONSIN

NEW YORK PUBLIC LIBRARY PICTURE COLLECTION

Though some of the jobs people had when your grandparents were your age have disappeared, others, like the fireman, the barber, and the ambulance driver, are still around.

As new inventions became popular, new jobs opened up. Telephone linemen became a familiar sight as the number of telephones nearly doubled from 1917 to 1927, to reach a total of 171,500,000. As new jobs opened up many women were able to find work outside the home for the first time. Why do you suppose all the workers here are women?

Working conditions have changed, too. The fans above the telephone switchboard may tell you something about what it was like to work in the hot summer. You may also wonder how well places were heated in the winter, or why the man is wearing a visor.

Where Woman's Service Looms Large

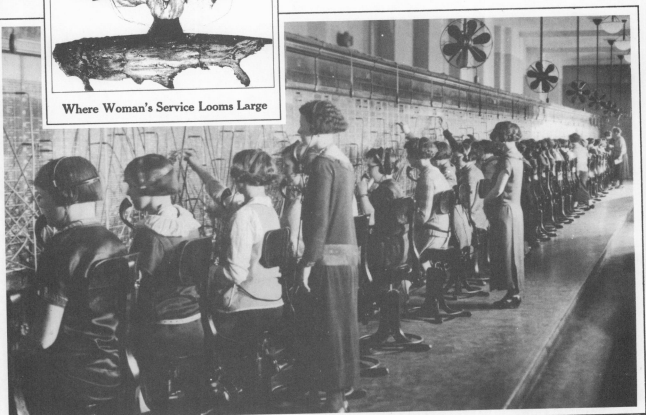

Some services, such as public transportation, have changed quite a bit since your grandparents were growing up. Streetcars have been replaced by subways and buses and, sometimes, by the monorail. Some "old fashioned" vehicles like the double-decker bus may be returning after a long absence, while inventions like traffic lights —which were new to your grandparents— have become so commonplace we cannot imagine what traffic would be like if they weren't there.

CHICAGO HISTORICAL SOCIETY

CALIFORNIA HISTORICAL SOCIETY

NEW YORK PUBLIC LIBRARY PICTURE COLLECTION

SUBWAY TRAINS COLLIDE, 17 HURT, SCORES TRAPPED

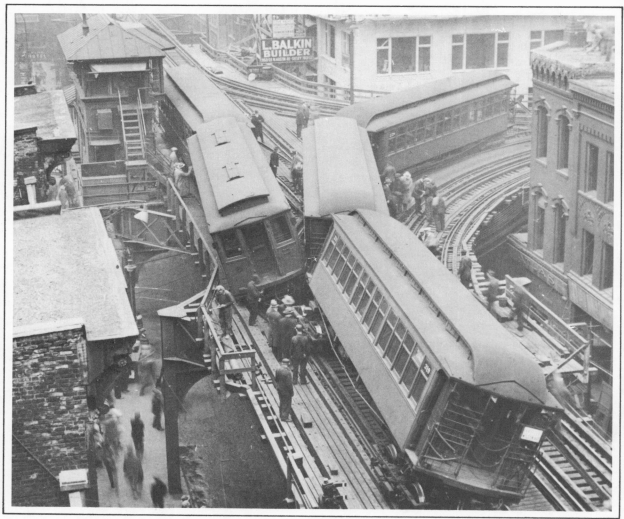

Just as today, when your grandparents were young there were accidents and crime in the streets.

2 SHOTGUN THUGS BAGGED IN CHASE

And, of course, there were policemen. Seeing policemen on horses may not seem strange for those of you who live in cities like New York, but seeing them on bikes or ice skates may be another matter! How do you think the job of a police officer has changed over the years?

In 1888, when women were hired to work in the New York Police Department, they were called police matrons and were assigned to police stations to deal with women who were arrested. In the 1920s they became known as policewomen and took on extra duties, such as working with children who were in trouble. It wasn't until 1973 that women won the right to become police officers with full responsibilities.

Most of these pictures suggest that everyday problems remain the same no matter where and when you live. Fire, crime, communication between people, sanitation, snow removal, and traffic, as well as health care, a clean water supply, and food distribution, are all common concerns when people live together.

ALFRED J. YOUNG COLLECTION, NEW YORK

Sometimes it's difficult for people to remember how problems were actually handled when they were growing up. They may forget what things were really like. These photographs will give you a hint that people's memories aren't always reliable. You've probably heard someone comment, "Traffic is getting terrible these days." After looking carefully at some of these photos, you might begin to wonder if things have really gotten worse.

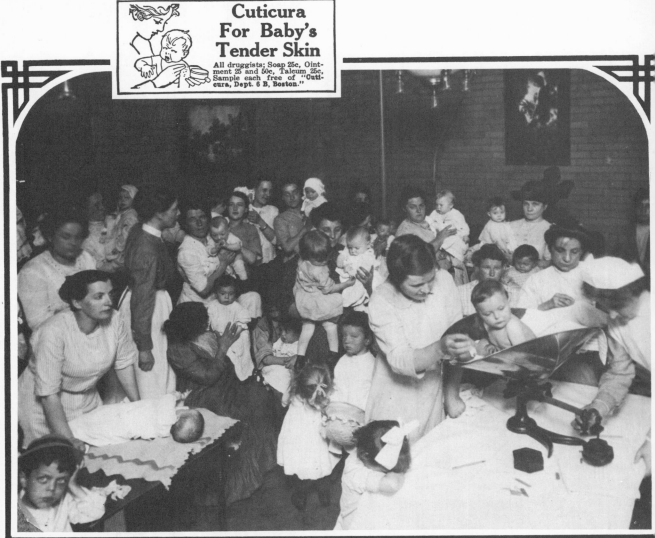

CHICAGO HISTORICAL SOCIE

Yₒu might ask your grandparents about health care for the elderly or for children. The visiting nurse and baby-care clinics are not new services. They were around even before your grandparents were born.

Services such as these were necessary because in those days most babies were born at home, rather than in a hospital. However, if your grandparents were born in a hospital, their mothers probably spent nine or ten days there instead of the three or four days women usually spend today.

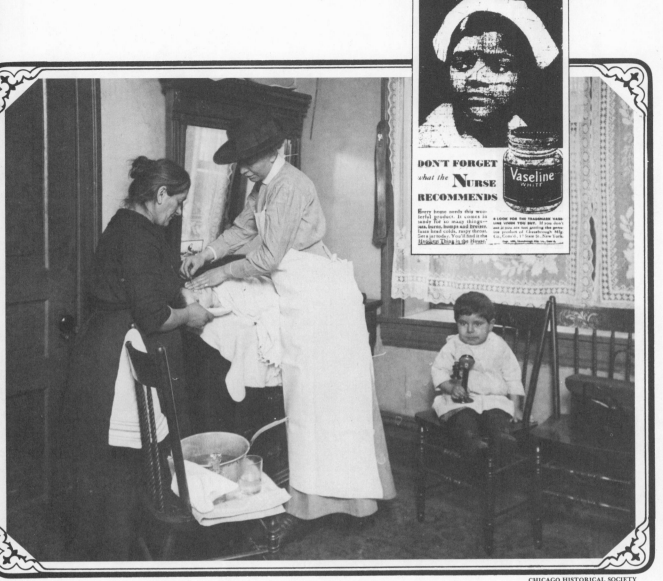

CHICAGO HISTORICAL SOCIETY

Many medical practices and problems have changed over the years. For example, the family doctor was a very special person when your grandparents were growing up and usually came to the house when people were sick.

Some major diseases like smallpox, which were particularly harmful to children, have almost disappeared.

How do you think parents tried to protect children from disease in those days? What things do people your grandparents' age remember about the family doctor?

PREVENTS INFLUENZA.

SANITAS
FLUID
SPRAYED ABOUT ROOMS
RAPIDLY
DESTROYS ALL DISEASE GERMS

Clean.
Fragrant.
Non-Poisonous.
Does not Stain Linen.
Oxygenates the Air

"SANITAS" Now Enjoys General Favour as a Disinfectant. Z4027

FLUIDS POWDER FUMIGATOR SOAPS &c.

THE "SANITAS" Co. LIMEHOUSE, LONDON. E.

MUSEUM OF THE CITY OF NEW YORK

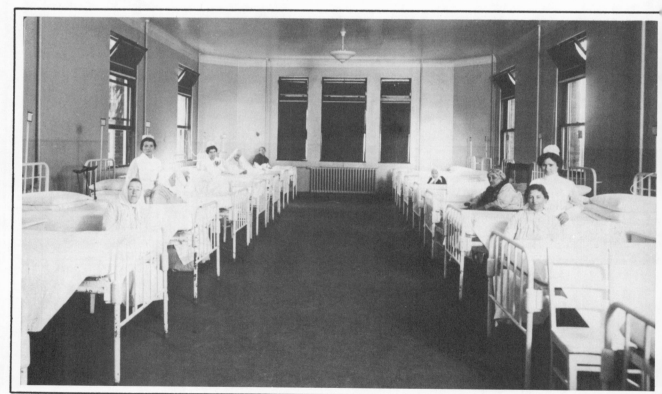

MONTEFIORE HOSPITAL AND MEDICAL CENTER

Then, as now, there were hospitals and visits to the dentist. What do you suppose the health inspections in schools were like?

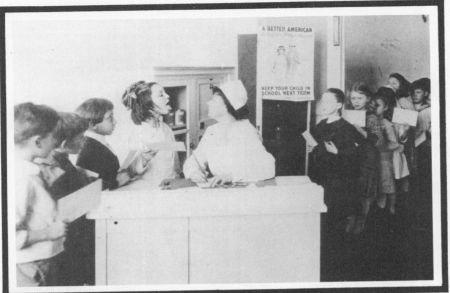

MUSEUM OF THE CITY OF NEW YORK

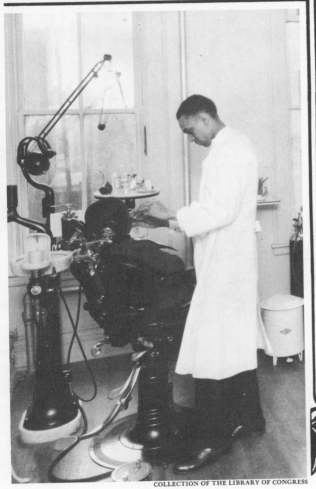

COLLECTION OF THE LIBRARY OF CONGRESS

Of course, people didn't worry about problems all the time. They found many ways to entertain themselves, some quite different from what people do today. If your grandparents were born around 1910, they would have been at least twelve years old before they had any radio programs to

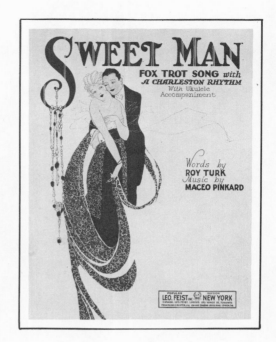

BERENICE ABBOTT, MUSEUM OF THE CITY OF NEW YORK

Film Ratings

In response to many requests from readers, THE LITERARY DIGEST is resuming a weekly rating of the new films. The ratings represent a consensus arrived at by analysis of the comment of screen reviewers throughout the country. They are not arbitrary ratings set by THE LITERARY DIGEST Screen Editor.

AAAA—"Mutiny on the Bounty"; "A Tale of Two Cities"; "Strike Me Pink."

AAA—"A Night at the Opera"; "So Red the Rose"; "Annie Oakley"; "Sylvia Scarlett"; "The Ghost Goes West."

AA—"Hands Across the Table"; "Frisco Kid"; "If You Could Only Cook."

The ratings are *AAAA*, Excellent; *AAA*, Good; *AA*, Acceptable, and *A*, Poor.

listen to, and they wouldn't have watched TV until they were thirty-five or forty years old! To them, the radio and phonograph were tremendously exciting inventions. They couldn't possibly have imagined that by the time they had grandchildren, there would be tape recorders, portable phonographs, TVs, and transistor radios.

Your grandparents couldn't have seen a movie with a sound track until 1927. Before "talkies," as they were called, people read captions on the screen and a local piano player supplied some background mood music while the movie ran.

BERENICE ABBOTT, MUSEUM OF THE CITY OF NEW YORK

Then, as now, there were many magazines and candy bars to choose from. You may recognize some of them. If you look closely at the cash register, you'll notice that someone has made a purchase with only a few pennies.

Some of the things people did then may seem strange to us today. World records for pole sitting were set and reset. Marathon or endurance dances were a big rage. The couple that could dance the longest—sometimes for weeks—could win lots of money. The rules allowed one partner to hold up the other while he or she slept, as long as the two kept on dancing. Some dancers collapsed. The marathon record was twenty-two weeks.

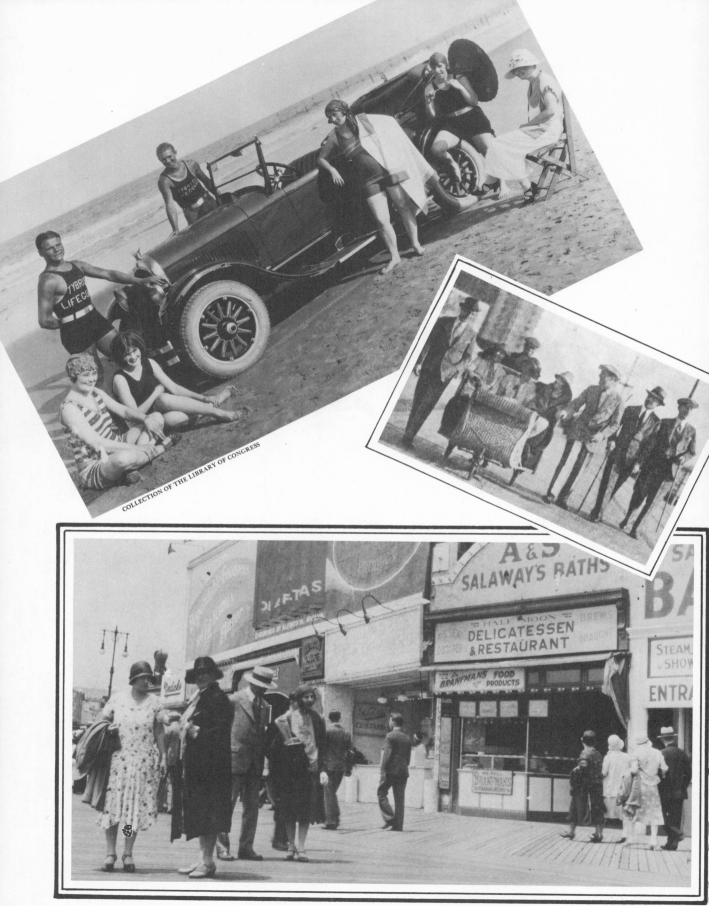

COLLECTION OF THE LIBRARY OF CONGRESS

COLLECTION OF CORAL FAMILY

There were many other ways people spent their time. They would go to the beaches or stroll along the ocean boardwalks. Sometimes they went to various sporting events.

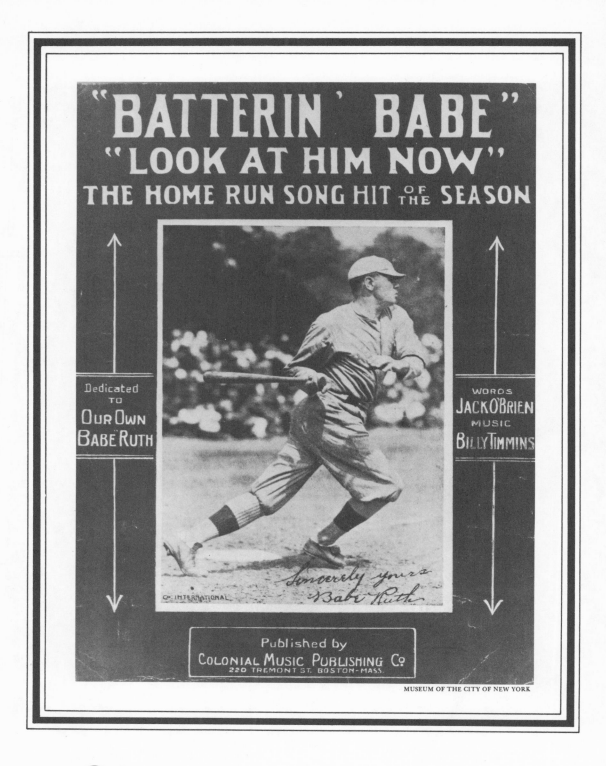

One of the great heroes of that day was Babe Ruth, a famous baseball player. Songs were written about him, and a candy bar was even named for him.

NEW YORK PUBLIC LIBRARY PICTURE COLLECTION

COLLECTION OF COHEN FAMILY

Other heroes were soldiers who fought in the First World War. When they came home, parades were held for them.

Parades were also held for explorers, politicians, visiting diplomats, and many others. Spectators lined the streets and threw confetti to welcome the celebrities.

See if you can find out what happened to these old-time heroes. What sort of people would get a ticker-tape parade today? What makes them heroes?

NBC PICTURE COLLECTION

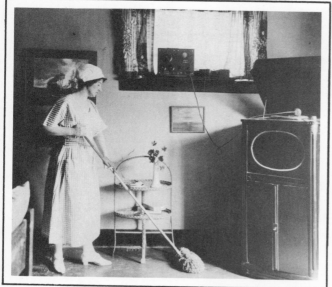

STATE HISTORICAL SOCIETY OF WISCONSIN

Some of the new inventions created new heroes or celebrities, like Will Rogers. Radio made it possible for stars like him to be heard all across the country, instead of by one audience at one live performance. Just as you and your friends might sit around the TV, your grandparents and their friends sat around the radio listening to the popular personalities, comedy shows, and mysteries. Or they followed their favorite radio soap operas.

CHICAGO HISTORICAL SOCIETY

As the actors read their parts into a microphone, sound-effects men made all the appropriate noises—a door opening, footsteps, thunder and lightning—any sound you can imagine. People would listen to the programs while they did the family chores. Today you can hear records of some of these old radio programs. Which do you think you would prefer—radio adventures or television? You might ask people who used to listen to radio and find out what they think.

If you have a tape recorder, you can try making your own sound effects or radio show.

Some things that seem very ordinary to us now were very exciting to your grandparents when they were growing up. As automobile manufacturers learned how to mass-produce cars, increasing numbers of Americans found they could afford to buy one. Families put their suitcases into auto trunks, tied them to the running boards or tops of cars, and set off to see the country.

COLLECTION OF GEISMAN FAMILY

But taking a trip in those days was **not** like it is today. Interstate highways didn't exist—the newest convenience for auto travel in your grandparents' day was the paved road. Top speed for cars in 1919 was about twenty miles per hour. By 1931 it was thirty-five or forty miles an hour. Bumpy, dusty trips didn't keep the automobile from becoming a very important feature of American life. In 1919 there were about 6,800,000 cars in use in the United States. Only ten years later, there were over 23,100,000. With the automobile came the now-familiar gas stations that dot towns and highways across the country. Ask some friends your grandparents' age whether they traveled by car when they were younger. If they did, where did they go, where did they stay, and how did they handle such misfortunes as flat tires?

Very few people had flown in an airplane when your grandparents were your age, and most never dreamed of doing so. In the earliest planes, pilots flew in uncovered cockpits, and stunt flying was popular at local fairs. Most planes were used to transport mail and newspapers. Only gradually did passenger service begin to develop.

EASTERN AIRLINES PHOTOGRAPHIC SERVICES

Comet-Like Flyer

Howard Hughes Rides Across U. S.
At 260 Miles an Hour

AT&T PHOTO CENTER

You can see what fares were like in the
early 1930s, but can you imagine what a
trip from New York to Miami must have
been like—it took almost fourteen hours
and made eleven stops along the way!

The Sunday Star.

WASHINGTON, D. C., SUNDAY MORNING, MAY 22, 1927—124 PAGES.

WITH DAILY EVENING EDITION

FIVE CENTS

PARIS WILDLY ACCLAIMS LINDBERGH

WELCOME RIVALS ARMISTICE DAY
SCENES AS HUGE THRONG IN MAD
RUSH GREETS FLYER ON ARRIVAL

"Well, I Did It," Grins "Lucky"
at End of Epoch-Making
Hop Across Atlantic.

CHEERING THOUSANDS EXULT
IN FRENCH CAPITAL STREETS

100,000 at Air Field Break Lines of
Soldiers as Youthful Pilot Lands
After 33½-Hour Flight.

BY EDWIN L. JAMES.

MEXICO INVOLVED AS BORAH ASSAILS NICARAGUAN POLICY

White House and Kellogg Point
to Aid Mexicans Are Giving
Sacasa Forces.

DON'T ACCUSE GOVERNMENT

Administration Stands Firm in
Its Support of the Diaz
Regime.

BELLANCA PLA[NE]
PARIS FLIGHT

[...]amberlin to Undertak[e]
[...] Hop Soon—Designe[r]
[...]its Backers.

San Francis[co]

LEADING NEWSPAPER

GREAT

Prince of Wales Leaps as Horse Stumbles;
Sprains Wrist, but Continues in the Hunt

Copyright, 1927, by The New York Times Company.
Special Cable to THE NEW YORK TIMES.

LONDON, Jan. 7.—The Prince of Wales met with another hunting accident today. He was out with the famous Quorn hunt in the neighborhood of Melton Mowbray when his horse stumbled at a difficult fence and fell. The Prince was able to jump clear, but in doing so badly sprained his left wrist and his wrist watch was smashed to atoms.

The horse, which had galloped away, was recaptured and restored to the Prince, who, although evidently in pain, pluckily remounted and completed the day's sport.

The Prince was not the only follower of the Quorn hunt to meet with an accident today. Violet, Duchess of Westminster, had [...] perience. Her ho[...] a complete som[...] juries.

Captain Gree[...] and his horse bro[...] Hornby had a sev[...] an arm and his col[...]

Less than a month [...]ing with the Quorn hou[...] Great Dalby, the Prince [...] unhorsed when his favorite [...] at a formidable hedge. [...] was thrown over the horse's [...] fell clear of the animal and ke[...] of the reins. In a moment he h[...] mounted and, covered with mud, [...]tinued to follow the chase.

THIS NEWSPAPER

Americans Win Honor

NEXT SUNDAY'S CHRONICLE

FOUNDED 1865

Many things such as international telephone service, so familiar to us now that we hardly think of them at all, made front-page headlines not very long ago.

The New York Times.

NEW YORK, SATURDAY, JANUARY 8, 1927.

TWO CENTS

CENT AMERICAN
nicle
FAIR WEATHER
SAN FRANCISCO
AND VICINITY
REG. U.S. PAT. OFF.
VOL. CXIII. NO. 119
1918

WAR OVER

Foe Signs Truce; Fighting Ceases On French Front

WASHINGTON, November 11.—The world war will end this morning at 6 o'clock, Washington time, 11 o'clock

armistice was signed by the German representatives. This announcement was made by

2:50 o'clock this morning.

was made verbally by an official

form:

ed. It was signed at 5

s will cease at

unced, u

howe

THE WEATHER
Fair and slightly warmer today!
tomorrow possibly rain or snow.
Temperature yesterday—Max. 31, min. 14.
For weather report on Page 20.

NEW YORK AND LONDON TALK FREELY, OPENING NEW RADIOPHONE SERVICE; FIRST PRIVATE CALL TO NEW YORK TIMES

LONDON HAILS NEW TIE

Radiophone Is Seen as Equal in Importance to Opening of Cable.

SERVICE IN GREAT DEMAND

Business Houses Are Among the First to Take Advantage of Quick Intercourse With Us.

SIMPLICITY STIRS WONDER

Reception Appears to Be Better Than That Experienced Here
—Talks Continued at Night.

Special Cable to The New York Times.

LONDON, Jan. 7.—London hailed today the first public telephonic conversations between New York and the British capital as an event of equal importance to the opening of the first transatlantic cable sixty-eight years ago or the first telephone eighteen years later.

So great was the demand for communication that at the last moment it was decided to keep the service open until 11 o'clock tonight (London Time).

31 CALLS ARE MADE IN DAY

Static Troubles Users Slightly, but Voices Usually Are Distinct.

TIME EXTENDED TO 6:30 P. M.

Sir Evelyn Murray and W. S. Gifford Call Phone New Link Between Nations.

SOCIAL AND BUSINESS CALLS

Two Advertisements Also Cross Ocean to The Times—Service Continues at 8:30 A. M. Today.

"Hello, London."

These two simple words, spanning the Atlantic on electric waves travel-ing with the speed of light, heralded the opening of the radio telephone be-tween New York and London yester-day morning, the most remarkable communication service yet devised by man.

His Honor of New York Telephones to London's Lord Mayor.

Times Wide World Photo.

$6,000,000 IN DEALS OVER RADIOPHONE

Wall Street Houses Talk to London on Foreign Exchange Transactions.

SCORE USE NEW SYSTEM

International Acceptance and Midland Banks Make Deal—A. T. & T. Stock Rises.

WALKER HAS HIS FUN OVER LONDON CHATS

"Just Like Talking to Albany," Is His Comment After Holding Conversations Across Sea.

GREETS THE LORD MAYOR

Tells an Editor They Had Better Be Confidential With Many Millions Listening In.

Mayor James J. Walker had two talks with London over the transatlan-tic radio telephone yesterday, and ap-parently enjoyed them.

THE WEATHER
Today: Rain and warmer
Tomorrow: Fair and colder
Temperatures Yesterday: Max., 44; Min., 34
Detailed Report on Page 21

NEW YORK Herald Tribune

LATE CITY EDITION

NRA MEMBER U.S. WE DO OUR PART

VOL. XCIII No. 31,797
(Copyright, 1933, New York Tribune Inc.)
WEDNESDAY, DECEMBER 6, 1933 ★★★★

TWO CENTS In Greater New York | THREE CENTS Within 200 Miles | FOUR CENTS Elsewhere

Prohibition Ends, Roosevelt Calls for Temperance; City and Nation Celebrate as Utah Votes In Repeal

National City Cuts Capital Stock and Aids R. F. C. Plan

James H. Perkins Reveals Plan to Reduce Common $46,500,000 and Sell $50,000,000 Preferred

Backs Roosevelt Recovery Program

Rumor Bank Proposed to Drop U. S. Charter Set at Rest; City Bank Farmers Stays Separate

James H. Perkins, chairman of the board of the National City Bank, announced yesterday a sweeping overhaul in the bank's capital structure including a reduction in the common stock from $124,000,000 to $77,500,000 through a cut in the par value from $20 to $12.50 a share, and the sale of $50,000,000 of preferred stock to the Reconstruction Finance Corporation.

In informing the stockholders of the proposed revamping of the capital setup, on which a vote will be taken at the annual meeting on January 9, Mr. Perkins took occasion to declare his and the directors' support of President Roosevelt's program.

Rumors Set at Rest

"Our directors," said Mr. Perkins, "feel that the bank should support the President of the United States in his program of strengthening the capital structure of the banks of the country and in his campaign to bring about business and industrial recovery. They feel also that we should accept the offer which the government has made to purchase preferred stock in national banks."

By thus lining up National City Bank, formerly the largest bank in the world and now second only to the Chase National Bank in size in this country, with the President's policies, Mr. Perkins set at rest rumors which have been in circulation in Wall Street in recent weeks. One of these widespread reports had it that National City Bank was going to give up its national charter and operate henceforth under the state charter of its trust affiliate so as to take itself out of reach of the national banking laws, which are considered more onerous and restrictive than those of New York State.

Mr. Perkins stated specifically moreover, that the City Bank Farmers Trust Company, ownership of which was acquired by National City in 1929, would be continued as a separate institution. Under the present arrangement the capital stock of the trust institution is held in trust for stockholders of the National City Bank. Recent reports had it that the bank and trust company would be merged.

Farmers to Join Reserve

The only changes that are being made in the way the City Bank Farmers Trust Company, which operated for more than 100 years under the name of Farmers' Loan and Trust Company, are that it will apply for membership in the Federal Reserve Bank of New York and will stand prepared to become a member of the Temporary Federal Deposit Insurance Fund and a stockholder in the Federal Deposit Insurance Corporation.

Mr. Perkins informed stockholders they could expect him to recommend to the board of directors the payment of a dividend of 25 cents a share on the common stock on February 1 1934. The ordinary date for payment of the dividend would be January 1 as the disbursement is to be made out of earnings in the final quarter of this year, but the existence of the preferred, it is understood, makes necessary the change in the dividend date. Current earnings of the bank are reported to be equal to approxi-

(Continued on page thirty-eight)

Reorganizes His Bank

Associated Press photo
James H. Perkins

12 N. Y. Banks To Sell Capital Notes to R. F. C.

Purchase by Government of $93,700,000 Issues Authorized Under Jones Plan

From the Herald Tribune Bureau

WASHINGTON, Dec. 5.—Authorization for the purchase of $93,700,000 worth of capital notes and preferred stock in twelve New York City banks was announced tonight by Jesse H. Jones, chairman of the Reconstruction Finance Corporation.

The announcement was regarded in official circles as an indication that some of the New York banks were disposed to "play ball" with the Administration. Mr. Jones said that none of the banks needed the additional funds, but that they were co-operating with the government's policy. However, the National City Bank, which proposes to sell $50,000,000 worth of preferred

(Continued on page thirty-eight)

Summary of Today's News

REPEAL

President proclaims repeal, calling on nation for temperance. Page 1
Liquor, no novelty here, flows at its usual tempo. Page 1
Jersey liquor-control bill voted by Assembly over veto. Page 1
Roosevelt's temperance plea. Page 1
United States opens gate to flow of rye from Canada. Page 2
New Yorkers add dry era to history with fitting toasts. Page 3
Chicago races with New York for first legal drink. Page 4
Mulrooney stays up until midnight issuing liquor permits. Page 5
Crowds in Times Square hail repeal with sober whisper. Page 6
Dearth of liquor supply slows repeal hilarity all over state. Page 7
Old restaurants here prepare to revive art of dining. Page 8
Crowds storm city's hotels at signal from Utah. Page 9
U. S. calls off 600 padlock cases in this district. Page 10
Utah clinches repeal in time to enjoy wet dinner. Page 11
Anti-Prohibition Association votes to disband December 31. Page 12
The President's proclamation. Page 12

WASHINGTON

Twelve New York banks to sell capital notes to R. F. C. Page 1
House subcommittee urges drastic changes in tax laws. Page 1
Text of Roosevelt rejection note to Hayti made public. Page 16
Glass charges Wall Street fought banking reforms. Page 16
Soft coal industry pledges support of N. R. A. program. Page 21

FOREIGN

Lindberghs off on 1,870-mile flight over south Atlantic. Page 1
German refugees estimated at 60,000, of whom 51,000 are Jews. Page 17
American interests defy Grau, plan to fight confiscation. Page 17
Mexico asks for debt and money talk at Montevideo parley. Page 18
Nazi pressure on United States press is urged at Berlin. Page 18
Irish demand for showdown sidestepped in Britain's reply. Page 19
Insull must leave Greece December 31, government decides. Page 44

SPORTS

Toronto hockey team swamps Americans, 9 to 1, at Garden. Page 29
Columbia starts planning for trip to Rose Bowl. Page 29
Harvard elects Gundlach; Yale names Clare Curtin. Page 29
Prentice sees America as strong Davis Cup contender. Page 30
Jazz Age wins by a head over Nyack at Jefferson Park. Page 31

CITY AND VICINITY

National City Bank cuts capital stock; aids R. F. C. plan. Page 1
N. R. A. board at Washington receives Loft objection. Page 14
Young sees welfare drive as prop to rugged individualism. Page 15
Painter depicts himself and wife twenty years older. Page 15
O'Brien's 1934 budget is called "fraud" by Untermyer. Page 16
Old cell block at Sing Sing criticized in prison handbook. Page 22
City approves purchase of Brooklyn college site. Page 23
President Roosevelt no Messiah, Dr. McGregor warns. Page 25
Second Tombs fugitive trapped by postman's uniform. Page 44
Drama and music. Page 24
Obituary articles. Page 23

NATIONAL

California business better, prices rising, Sullivan finds. Page 16
Southern pair wins Hilliard bridge trophy at Cincinnati. Page 20
Alabama jury is deadlocked after long argument. Page 44
Huey Long's choice is elected amid show of arms. Page 44

EDITORIALS AND FEATURES

Editorials. Page 26
Today and Tomorrow, by Walter Lippmann. Page 23
Books and Things, by Lewis Gannett. Page 25
The Conning Tower, by F.P.A. Page 25
Radio programs. Page 42
Fashion and food news. Page 20
The Bridge Table. Page 20
H. T. Webster's cartoon. Page 31
"Mr. and Mrs." Page 43
Nature story. Page 20
Cross-word puzzle. Page 43
Detailed weather report. Page 21
Today's calendar of events. Page 21

MARINE AND SHIPPING

Incoming, outgoing ships. Page 22
Trans-Atlantic shipping men meet today in London. Page 22
Army and Navy orders. Page 42

FINANCIAL MARKETS

	Page		Page
Stock quotations	34	Cable rep'ts	40
Wall St comment	33	Over counter	38
Bond dealings	36	Produce	41
Foreign exchange	40	Grain	41
Financial notices	39	Produce Ex.	41
Business records	38	Other cities	39
Curb exchange	40	Cotton	41

Stock market scores good advance as volume increases. Page 33
Baker reveals Manhattan Co. confidential data. Page 33
Dates on insurance convention valuation of securities changed. Page 33

Advertising Index—Page 2

"Better Type"

WINE SALESMEN, experienced, for restaurant, wholesale and retail trade. Only men of highest caliber need apply. State age, qualifications and past experience. D 464 Herald Tribune, Downtown.

"We were very well pleased with the results. The applicants were the better type of salesmen, from whom we selected several," says the above advertiser.

To secure a selection of high grade sales help, tell your story to the daily readers of the Herald Tribune. Phone PEnnsylvania 6-4000.

Lindberghs Off to Brazil From Africa

Airplane Rises at 2 A. M. Upon Tenth Attempt; Moon Lights Atlantic for 1,870-Mile Flight

Wife Sends Radio: 'Everything O. K.'

German Air Base Ship and Two Small Islands Offer Havens on Way

By The Associated Press

BATHURST, Gambia, British West Africa, Dec. 6 (Wednesday).—Colonel and Mrs. Charles A. Lindbergh, homeward bound after five months of air travel abroad, took off over the South Atlantic at 2 a. m. today, Greenwich time (9 p. m. Tuesday, Eastern standard time). They were expected to land after about fourteen hours of flight at Natal, Brazil, 1,870 miles distant, or at some other Brazilian port.

Wife Reports "Everything O. K."

A message radioed from the Lindbergh plane to Bahia, Brazil, and relayed to Pan-American Airways in New York reported the craft's position an hour after the takeoff as 12:07 north, 17:56 west, or 115 miles at sea.

Mrs. Lindbergh reported "everything O. K." She fixed a schedule for future communications, saying she would report the progress of the flight every fifteen minutes and would give their position every half hour.

At 12:30 a. m., E. S. T., Mrs. Lindbergh reported: "Position 9:50 north 20:15 west. Course 224 true. Visibility ten miles. Position 446 miles southwest of Bathurst, speed 100 knots. Altitude 1,200 feet. Wind 30 degrees (off the tail.)"

The Pan-American operators at Bahia reported to New York that Mrs. Lindbergh was sending "like a professional," and that her signals were coming "very clearly." She reported, however, that she was getting "a little static" on messages picked up by the plane.

The Lindberghs had made at least nine futile attempts to lift their heavily loaded monoplane from the waters of Gambia River after being held there for four days with a dead calm preventing the ship from rising. Severeal times they had reduced the gasoline load and removed other items from the plane's cargo, but to no avail. A fresh-

(Continued on page eighteen)

Liquor Flows Here at Its Usual Tempo

Experience No Novelty, so All Take It Easy; Supplies Run Short Early in the Evening

Police Seize Score In Cordial Shops

Warehouses Start Deliveries at Night; Stock To Be Plentiful Today

The passing of national prohibition and the return of legal liquor evoked a mild celebration around the town last night. There was no novelty about drinking, and so the citizenry, by and large, remained at home.

Enough celebrants sallied forth, however, to fill the hotels with merrymakers. The festivities were slow in getting under way because of delays in delivering liquor, but at midnight the situation was well in hand.

No Shortage Today

Deliveries continued all night. Today there will be no shortage.

There was no doubt that illegal drinking showed a marked decline. The high class speakeasies almost uniformly declined to serve liquor, and the low class places were in decided awe of the law. Even so, it will take time to adjust New York's drinking habits. Edward P. Mulrooney, chairman of the State Alcoholic Beverage Control Board, approved 800 licenses of various types for the city yesterday, although the names of licensees were not made public. Mr. Mulrooney thinks he may finish the licensing task in two weeks—by Christmas, anyway.

A decent restraint marked the first hours of licensed liquors. Patrons were encouraged to sip instead of gulp. The temperance movement was helped along by the cession of many speakeasies and cordial shops to lay low for a while. Police had instructions to raid all speakeasies, cordial shops and illicit liquor places of any description. At midnight about a dozen cordial shops and several speakeasies had been raided.

Instructions for the anti-speakeasy-cordial shop drive had been given by Police Commissioner James S. Bolan to his inspectors assembled at Police Headquarters for the occasion. Last night Chief Inspector John O'Brien sent out an additional instruction that police were not to "interfere with the lawful sale or transportation of alcoholic beverages."

Police Start Liquor Raids

When this order came over the police teletype, Inspector John J. Seery at the East Sixty-Seventh Street Station, was instructing fourteen of his plainclothes men to go out and raid every place caught violating the new liquor regulations. The men went out in pairs and soon they began to return in pairs, bringing prisoners with them.

The doubtful distinction of being the first man arrested for selling liquor without a license went to Jack Level, who was taken in custody in a cordial shop at 1499 Third Avenue, charged with selling contraband to detectives. About 1,000 bottles of wines were confiscated in the shop.

Louis Bruno was arrested in a cordial

(Continued on page eleven)

The First to Salute the New Era of Legal Drinking

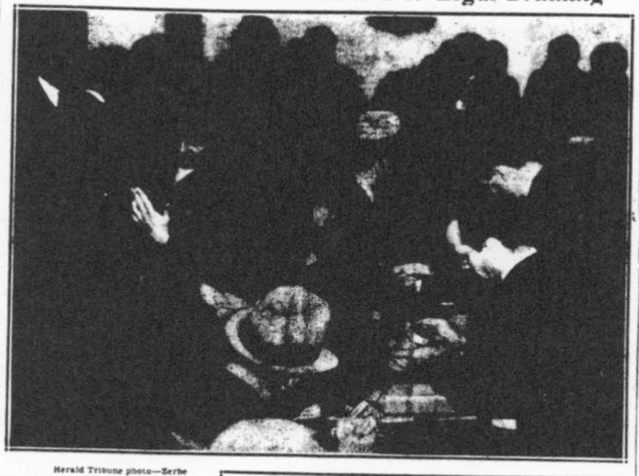

Herald Tribune photo—Zerbe
Part of the crowd that surged into Bloomingdale's to lay in a supply of wet goods as soon as news of Utah's action was received here

New Tax Yield Of 237 Million Asked in House

Higher Income, Dividend and Holding Co. Levies Urged by Subcommittee

From the Herald Tribune Bureau

WASHINGTON, Dec. 5.—Drastic changes in tax laws, estimated to add $237,000,000 a year to the Federal government's revenues, were recommended today by a subcommittee of the House Ways and Means Committee in a tax revision program which it submitted to the full committee.

Increased income taxes, in addition to other important changes, are favored by the subcommittee. Later the group will make additional recommendations. The Ways and Means Committee will review the subcommittee's report in hearings which will begin soon.

The suggestions for increased taxes are looked on here as serving to bring home to the public the fact that the enormously increased expenditures of the government for various purposes will entail added burdens.

The recommendations of the subcommittee, which are referred to as a preliminary report, call for increased surtax rates on incomes and a normal rate of 4 per cent on all income, instead of the present 4 per cent on the first $4,000 net income and 8 per cent on more than $4,000. It is recommended that dividends be subjected to a greater income tax. Heavy taxes are recommended against personal holding companies. The report refers to such concerns as a "scheme of the incorporated pocketbooks."

The recommendations of the subcommittee would provide for the following revenue:

Through changes in the normal and surtax rates and credits against

(Continued on page sixteen)

Benjamin De Casseres, author and bon vivant, sips his Scotch as he receives the flash from Utah over a special wire in the Waldorf-Astoria Herald Tribune photo—Acme

Roosevelt's Temperance Plea

From the Herald Tribune Bureau

WASHINGTON, Dec. 5.—President Roosevelt's appeal to the nation to co-operate with the government in its administration of liquor control and to avoid "the curse" of excessive drinking is contained in the following excerpt from his repeal proclamation:

Furthermore, I enjoin upon all citizens of the United States and upon others resident within the jurisdiction thereof, to co-operate with the government in its endeavor to restore greater respect for law and order, by confining such purchases of alcoholic beverages as they may make solely to those dealers or agencies which have been duly licensed by state or Federal license.

Observance of this request, which I make personally to every individual and every family in our nation, will result in the consumption of alcoholic beverages which have passed Federal inspection, in the break-up and eventual destruction of the notoriously evil illicit liquor traffic, and in the payment of reasonable taxes for the support of government and thereby in the superseding of other forms of taxation.

I call specific attention to the authority given by the Twenty-first Amendment to the government to prohibit transportation or importation of intoxicating liquors into any state in violation of the laws of such state.

I ask the whole-hearted co-operation of all our citizens to the end that this return of individual freedom shall not be accompanied by the repugnant conditions that obtained prior to the adoption of the Eighteenth Amendment and those that have existed since its adoption. Failure to do this honestly and courageously will be a living reproach to us all.

I ask especially that no state shall by law or otherwise authorize the return of the saloon either in its old form or in some modern guise.

The policy of the government will be to see to it that the social and political evils that have existed in the pre-prohibition era shall not be revived nor permitted again to exist. We must remove forever from our midst the menace of the bootlegger and such others as would profit at the expense of good government, law and order.

I trust in the good sense of the American people that they will not bring upon themselves the curse of excessive use of intoxicating liquors, to the detriment of health, morals and social integrity.

The objective we seek through a national policy is the education of every citizen towards a greater temperance throughout the nation.

Jersey Liquor Control Bill Voted By Assembly Over Moore's Veto

By a Staff Correspondent

TRENTON, N. J., Dec. 6 (Wednesday).—The New Jersey House of Assembly today passed the State Liquor Control Bill by a vote of 32 to 21 over the veto of Governor A. Harry Moore, who had contended that the measure was unconstitutional. The bill was then sent to the Senate.

Governor Moore's veto had left the state in confusion as to the regulation of the liquor traffic legalized by repeal of the Eighteenth Amendment.

In his message to the Republican-controlled Assembly the Democratic Governor said he would approve the bill proposed by the commission headed by Thomas N. McCarter, most of the sections of which were scrapped by the Legislature. He said he was not opposed to D. Frederick Burnett, Republican lawyer, of Newark, who was named in the Legislature's bill as State Liquor Control Commissioner.

"I am constrained to return without my approval Assembly Bill 611 despite the clamor that such action on my part may result in some temporary confusion as to the sale of liquor," Governor Moore said in his message. He said that for the thirteen years of Federal prohibition liquor had been sold illegally and that even today "it is generally understood" that hard liquor is sold in most of the places where beer is dispensed.

Therefore, he said, he did not believe that "we should be concerned over the brief delay incident to overriding my veto or amending the bill."

The Governor's veto was based on his contention that the control act was unconstitutional in several phases. He reached his decision to veto the bill after a series of conferences with Senator Emerson L. Richards, Republican, of Atlantic County, President of the upper house; Senator Clifford R. Powell, of Burlington, majority leader in the Senate, and Assemblyman Herbert J. Pascoe, of Union, Speaker of the House.

He had hoped that the state would have a control act when repeal became effective, but contended that the measure was so defective that he was

(Continued on page ten)

BIG CELEBRATION TONIGHT, Dinner and Supper. Cocoanut Grove, Park Central Hotel, 56th St. and 7th Avenue.—Advt.

Liquor Dec. 15 on Railroads

None of the railroads touching New York will attempt to serve liquor in dining cars or chair cars before December 15. Both the Pennsylvania and the New York Central have Federal licenses, but they must get licenses from the various states they pass through before wine lists may become a part of Pullman car literature. The Long Island Railroad has no diners.

HOTEL BREVOORT: Special REPEAL DINNER tonight at regular price of $1.50 per cover. Music. STuyvesant 9-4674.—Advt.

45,549 Tipplers Died in Dry Era

WASHINGTON, Dec. 5 (UP).—During the prohibition years from 1920 to 1932, 45,549 persons died from alcoholism, the Census Bureau reported today. The totals by years were: 900 in 1920; 1,611 in 1921; 2,467 in 1922; 3,148 in 1923; 3,158 in 1924; 3,494 in 1925; 4,109 in 1926; 4,372 in 1927; 4,627 in 1928; 4,220 in 1929; 4,156 in 1930; 3,926 in 1931, and 3,045 in 1932.

Christmas Cruise, Dec. 22: 10 Days $90, to Nassau, Miami, Havana: All Expenses Included. Munson Lines, 67 Wall.—Advt.

Dry Era Over As 36th State Acts at 5:32

President Issues Appeals to U. S. To Be Moderate in Exercising New Freedom and to Bar Saloon

$212,000,000 Tax Levies Rescinded

13-Year Experiment Sent 144,000 to Prisons, Cost Hundreds of Lives

By Theodore C. Wallen

WASHINGTON, Dec. 5.—National prohibition came to an end at 5:32 p. m. today, Eastern standard time, with the ratification of the repeal amendment by a state convention in Utah. The official word was flashed to Washington by telegraph in three minutes, and the adoption of the substitute amendment was formally proclaimed at 5:49½ p. m. by William Phillips, Acting Secretary of State.

President Roosevelt, at 6:55 p. m., issued a proclamation repealing four special taxes yielding an estimated $212,000,000 a year and directing a "personal" appeal to all citizens to exercise their restored "individual freedom" in a spirit of temperance.

The President called for whole-hearted public co-operation to restore greater respect for law and order, to protect the dry states and to insure the banishment of the bootlegger, the saloon, the illicit liquor traffic and the "repugnant conditions" of prohibition and pre-prohibition days.

Use of Legal Liquor Only Urged

Declaring his confidence in the good sense of the American people not to bring upon themselves "the curse of excessive use of intoxicating liquors," the President warned that the return of the old conditions would be "a living reproach to us all." Individuals and families were advised that they could contribute to the spirit of lawfulness by consuming only such alcoholic beverages as had passed Federal inspection, had paid reasonable taxes for the support of the government and were dispensed through regularly licensed dealers.

The President's proclamation ended a thirteen-year experiment which cost $127,000,000 for enforcement, killed 99 dry agents, wounded 561, killed 175 civilians at hands of agents and in the last six years sent 144,000 persons to prison for 71,000 years.

Bar on Saloon Urged

The President asked especially that the states authorize no return of the saloon in any form. He signed the proclamation in the privacy of his study and in the presence of only Stephen T. Early, one of his secretaries. The special taxes which it automatically repealed, as of dates varying between January 1 and July 1, 1934, are the levies on gasoline, dividends, capital stock and excess profits which were adopted in the extraordinary session of Congress to help finance the national recovery program.

Never before had an amendment to the Constitution of the United States been blotted out, as was the Eighteenth Amendment, by the substitution today of the Twenty-first Amendment.

Aside from its moral influence, the only legal effect of the President's proclamation was to set the wheels in motion for these tax repealers, which are to be followed by liquor taxes estimated to yield the Federal government a net gain of about $300,000,000 a year. Even the proclamation of the Acting Secretary of State, issued more than an hour earlier and with a greater show of ceremony, was a mere formality.

Sam Thurman's Vote Decisive

Pennsylvania and Ohio having filed the thirty-fourth and thirty-fifth ratifications of the Twenty-first Amendment to the Federal Constitution during the day, it was the deciding vote of one Sam Thurman in the Utah repeal convention which terminated the prohibition experiment after 13 years, 10 months and 19 days.

Through an unprecedented radio link between the State Department and the state voting the final ratifi-

THE CHICAGO DAILY NEWS

54TH YEAR—39. THURSDAY, FEBRUARY 14, 1929. FORTY-EIGHT PAGES. FINAL EDITION

MASSACRE 7 OF MORAN GANG

HAFFA CHANGES HIS MIND; WILL FIGHT PRISON

Owes It to Friends, He Says; Makes Bond, Prepares Appeal.

MAY STAY IN COUNCIL

After a night in the county jail, Ald. Titus Haffa of the 43d ward, facing now on $25,000 bail, has changed his mind and decided he will fight against going to federal prison to serve a two-year sentence for bootlegging. He had announced yesterday that he would give up without a struggle and leave with a bunch of prisoners scheduled to start for Leavenworth tomorrow night. Today he declared he'd go to the United States Supreme court if necessary to stay the "rap."

Haffa went free on bail this afternoon after Judge Walter C. Lindley had appeared in at the federal building. The bond was put up by a security company. It assured Haffa's release for at least a few months while his appeal is being made.

Haffa, who refused in the changed attitude to say whether he would resign from the city council and withdraw from the aldermanic race, might have stuck out his chin definitely as he made the announcement in the office of Warden Edward J. Fogarty; but he was deterred by a stiff neck which he blamed on conditions in the jail.

Changes His Mind.

Haffa's change of mind was made shortly after he had conferred for some time with his attorneys, Robert M. Woodward and Theodore Levin, with assistant state's attorneys, and a friend, Edward Zdaarer, precinct captain in Haffa's ward organization.

"To I look like a crushed man?" the alderman, who was sentenced recently for conspiracy to violate the pro-

TWO OF VICTIMS AND SCENE OF LATEST GANGSTER OUTBREAK

STAYS GIVEN 2 OF 3 KILLERS DUE TO DIE TONIGHT

KILLING SCENE TOO GRUESOME FOR ONLOOKERS

View of Carnage Proves a Strain on Their Nerves.

IS LIKE A SHAMBLES

It's too much to tell. You go into the door marked "S-M-C Cartage company." You see a bunch of big men talking with restrained excitement in the cigarette smoke. You go through another door, back of the front office. You go between two tires parked trucks in the garage.

Then you almost stumble over the head of the first man, with a clean gray felt hat still placed at the precise angle of gangster tenderness.

The dull yellow light of a long daytime shows dark rivulets of blood heading down to the drain that was meant for the water from washed cars. There are six of the red streams from six heads. The bodies—four of them well dressed in civilian clothes—two of them with their legs crossed as they willed to fall.

It's too much, as you crowd on past the roadster with bullet holes in it to the big truck behind.

Too Much for the Dog.

You look at the truck. It is something to look at because the men were facing it. Its jacked up, with one wheel off. You look and the big man called "chauffeur" looks and a crowd gathers, and then it gets too much for the pillow d'g paw had faded to notice lying under the truck, tied to it by a sharp yellow rope.

It gets too much for the big brown and gray pollice dog and he gives crazy fits barks, he howls, he snarls, showing wicked while teeth in bright red gums.

The crowd backs away. The dog it why, once more and subsides.

Your thoughts snap with a crack

VICTIMS ARE LINED AGAINST WALL; ONE VOLLEY KILLS ALL

Assassins Pose as Policemen; Flee in "Squad Car" After Fusillade; Capone Revenge for Murder of Lombardo, Officers Believe.

Seven Moran-O'Banion gangsters were lined up against the wall of a beer-distributing point at 2122 North Clark street at 10:30 o'clock today. Four men, two of them in police uniforms, stood before them, armed with machine guns and sawed-off shot guns. The leader of the execution squad barked an order and the seven fell, six dying at once, the seventh three hours later.

The execution, carried out with the precision of a Mexican firing squad, is charged by the police to the Capone-Lombardo interests. Greatest in point of numbers, it was also the most cold-blooded in the history of Chicago's gangland slaughter.

The dead, as identified by the police, were:

GUSENBERG, PETER, notorious gunman for the O'Banion-Weiss-Drucci-Moran mob.

GUSENBERG, FRANK, brother of Peter. He died after the others were killed, but refused to talk, though conscious.

WEINSHANK, AL, north side "alky" peddler.

MAY, JOHN, 1249 West Madison street, a 30-a-week mechanic, apparently killed to silence him.

CLARK, JOHN, brother-in-law of George ("Bugs") Moran, leader of the gang.

DAVIS, ARTHUR, west side racketeer.

FOSTER, FRANK, hoodlum.

A second theory advanced by federal prohibition agents was that the massacre was perpetrated by a band of rum runners from Detroit and known to put off the blood gang for

War to Finish Russell's Plan

THE BETTMAN ARCHIVE

Major events that might have excited or outraged people when your grandparents were growing up are now "history" and unfamiliar to children growing up today.

One time well remembered by those who lived through it is a period called the Depression. While some people had jobs, many men and women spent day after day searching for work. When everything else failed, they turned to occupations like selling apples on street corners.

Many families in the Depression had to do without things that we use all the time—toothpaste, toilet paper, newspapers, magazines, soft drinks, potato chips, rubber bands, paper clips, cars, commercial laundering, Christmas cards, and candy bars. When money was short, even electric lights weren't used much. Perhaps only one light in a home was turned on.

When they could no longer afford to pay rent, some people became squatters, building groups of shacks in parks and open spaces across the country. They often shared food with one another.

Anyone who grew up in the 1930s can tell you what life was like then and how different people managed to live through this difficult time.

Politicians argued about ways to end the Depression. Franklin Delano Roosevelt became President in a campaign that centered on the problems of the economy. After he was elected, many politicians running for office advertised that they agreed with him, just as today politicians advertise their opinions on TV, radio, or sound trucks.

If you're interested in politics, you might try to find out what problems the politicians used to debate about and whether the problems or the solutions proposed then were different from those discussed today.

ARTICLES OF COMMON USE
ALARM CLOCK
CAN OPENER
MINIATURE CAMERA
TAPE MEASURE AND SAFETY PIN
TOOTHBRUSH AND TOOTH POWDER
HAT BY LILLY DACHÉ
MICKEY MOUSE PLASTIC CUP
SAFETY RAZOR AND BLADES

MATERIALS OF OUR DAY
FABRICS OF ASBESTOS AND GLASS
CARBON AND STAINLESS STEELS
ANTHRACITE COAL
PLASTIC AIRPLANE CONTROL PULLEY

MISCELLANEOUS ITEMS
SILVER DOLLAR, HALF DOLLAR
    AND OTHER U.S. COINS
ELECTRIC WALL SWITCH AND LAMP SOCKET
THE ALPHABET, IN HANDSET TYPE
SPECIAL MESSAGES FROM SCIENTISTS
    AND WRITERS
VIEWER FOR EXAMINING MICROFILM
    AND NEWSREEL FILM

MICROFILM SEQUENCES
THE LORD'S PRAYER IN 300 LANGUAGES
DICTIONARIES, STANDARD AND SLANG
PHOTOGRAPHS OF FACTORIES
    AND PRODUCTION LINES
ARROWSMITH BY SINCLAIR LEWIS AND *GONE
    WITH THE WIND* BY MARGARET MITCHELL
PHOTOGRAPHS OF POKER PLAYING; A GOLF
    MATCH; A BASEBALL GAME
ASSORTED MAGAZINES
ASSORTED COMIC STRIPS, ATLASES,
    TECHNICAL MANUALS

NEWSREELS
SPEECH BY PRESIDENT
    FRANKLIN D. ROOSEVELT
SCENES FROM HOWARD HUGHES'
    ROUND-THE-WORLD FLIGHT
JESSE OWENS WINNING THE 100-METER DASH IN
    THE OLYMPIC GAMES OF 1936
THE BOMBING OF CANTON IN THE WAR
    BETWEEN CHINA AND JAPAN
THE UNITED STATES NAVY ON MANEUVERS
A FASHION SHOW IN MIAMI, FLORIDA
PREVIEW SCENES OF
    THE NEW YORK WORLD'S FAIR OF 1939

This book gives you some idea of what happened and what life was like when your grandparents were your age, but different photographs and events might have been selected—because everyone sees the world in his or her own way.

In 1939 a time capsule was buried in the ground, to be dug up five thousand years later. It contained objects selected to reveal what life was like at that time. The objects chosen probably tell you just as much about what people *thought* was important then.

If you were to ask yourself, "What will *I* tell *my* grandchildren life was like when I was their age?" there would be so many things to show and so many events to describe that you couldn't possibly cover everything. You would have to choose, just as the people did who buried the time capsule.

You could put together your own "time capsule" in an album. The photographs you choose and the way you describe what life was like when the photos were taken could make a very interesting collection. You might find it very difficult to decide what to include and what to leave out. As you make your decisions, try checking with some friends to see whether they'd make the same choices you would. Perhaps you'll have some debates about why to choose one thing or another. And perhaps you'll find that although you can understand your friends' reasons, you would still choose something they would want left out.

If you do make a scrapbook "time capsule," you may be surprised when you look back at it in a year or two. Things that seem of great importance now might seem strangely unimportant later. You may find you've changed your ideas or not remembered things quite the way they actually happened. Yet the memories you have make you a talking history book with many interesting events to relate. Since people your grandparents' age are talking history books, too, the next time someone says, "when I was your age," if you ask some good questions, you may hear stories from the past others have never heard.

Ann Cook and Herb Mack are both Assistant Professors at Brooklyn College, where Marilyn Gittell is Associate Provost and Professor of Political Science. Mr. Mack and Ms. Cook are also co-directors of the Community Resources Institute, a teacher-training and curriculum-development center in New York City. The three have worked in New York public schools for a number of years. They are co-authors of *City Life,* a study of urban living in the late 19th century, and have individually published several other books for children as well as adults.